Tunisian

47 Patterns And Stitches for You to Try

Introduction

Tunisian crochet is a cross between knitting and crochet, when you look at a piece of Tunisian crochet you will notice that it has its own look. Tunisian crochet does not have as many variations in stitches as knitting or crocheting. There is no double or treble crochet stitches and it is much easier to do than knitting.

This crochet technique is known by several different names; Afghan stitch, Sheppard's knitting, Railway knitting, and Tricot work to name a few. The stitch incorporates both knitting and crocheting techniques and yields a heavy fabric that is perfect for winter warmth.

The history of this stitch is not well documented but it is believed to have come from Afghanistan, hence the Afghan stitch, and at some point it made its way into Tunisia and then to the west and north. Today this stitch is used by everyone and the resulting fabrics have a look all their own.

Several variations of stitch are used in Tunisian crochet, casting on and casting off are techniques known to knitters and they are also used in Tunisian crochet. Those who crochet will notice that that the stitch is pulled through the loop and left on the hook like a knit stitch. Knitters will notice that the work is not turned, it is worked on the same side at all times.

Those who have a background in crochet will find this stitch easy to master. It is less complicated than most crochet stitches and the fabric works up faster than traditional crochet. Compared to knitting, Tunisian crochet is twice as fast to work resulting in names like the mile-a-minute stitch.

Tunisian crochet begins with a regular crochet chain, then it is worked forward, then back without turning the fabric. The yarn is worked onto the hook on the forward pass, then worked off of the hook on the return or backward pass. After learning just three simple stitches it is possible to create an endless parade of items.

Tunisian crochet has fancy and simple stitches. The simple stitch creates a very nice grid pattern similar to a waffle weave or thermal. The grid pattern created is great for embroidery, the fabric made could be used for embroidered throws, Afghans, and items like decorative throw pillows.

Choosing to learn Tunisian crochet broadens your skill set and introduces you to new types of projects that would be difficult for crochet or knitting alone. The Tunisian stitch can be worked in the round using a special tool and the result is a pair of great mittens or wrist warmers, and beautiful cowls and leg warmers.

More advanced fancy Tunisian stitches can be used to decorate and add style to items created with the simple stitch. The fancy stitches add a bit of interest to projects but the common Tunisian stitches also deliver interesting and eye catching style on their own. Beginners will be surprised at the wide array of items they can create with only three stitches.

The patterns included in this book do not use any fancy stitches, only common stitches, this makes it easy for a beginner to create a project the first time they try. Many stitches are considered easy enough for beginners and each stitch adds detail to the project. Even some 18th century tapestry was created with the simple Tunisian stitch.

Before you dive into Tunisian crochet you will need the proper tools. A basket or other type of container to hold the yarn, hooks, and projects you are creating. An Afghan hook, a yarn needle, measuring tape, and anything else the patterns require. Other types of hooks exist but they are not used for any of the patterns in this book.

Chapter 1 – Learning Tunisian Crochet

Tunisian crochet uses a hook called an Afghan hook. The Afghan hook is almost as long as a knitting needle and it has a crochet hook on one end and a block on the other. The block is there to keep the stitches on the hook. Other types of Afghan/Tunisian hooks are available for different types of stitches or projects, but for a beginner, all that is needed is an Afghan hook.

Tunisian crochet uses techniques from crochet and knitting to produce a thick, warm, fabric. As a beginner, you will use simple Tunisian stitches to create ten different beginner projects. Before moving on to the pattern chapter, practice the stitches here until you are comfortable with them.

Foundation and Preparation Rows

The foundation and preparation rows are the first two rows of any project. To begin, make a loop around the hook and pull the yarn through the loop using the hook. Now you have a slip knot on the hook. Continue to grab the yarn and pull it through the loop on the hook until you have about fifteen chain stitches.

The fifteen chain stitches are the preparation row, the foundation row builds on this preparation row. The foundation row begins in the second stitch from the hook. Do not turn the work, put the hook through the second stitch from the hook and leave the new loop on the hook. Put the hook through the next stitch in the chain and pull the yarn through the stitch, leave the new loop on the hook next to the first loop. Continue this until all of the stitches are on the hook and you have come to the end of the preparation row.

The stitches you have just completed are now on the hook, this is called casting on, and it creates the foundation row, just like in knitting. The next step is the return row, this row will remove the loops from the hook.

Return Row

Now without turning the work you will work back, this is the return row. Chain 1 then yarn over and pull the hook through two stitches on the hook. Repeat this until only one loop remains on hook.

Forward Row

Next is the forward row. On the last loop, yarn over and pull through the loop leaving a new loop on the hook. Without turning the work, insert the hook into the next vertical stitch, yarn over, and then pull through leaving a loop on the hook. Continue this until you have fifteen loops on the hook.

Finishing Off

When all of the rows are complete and you have finished on a *return row*; insert the hook into the chain stitch of the previous row. Now yarn over and pull through. Cut the yarn and weave the end of it into the last row using a yarn needle. A yarn needle is a needle with an eye large enough to thread yarn.

If the row ends on a *forward row* the finish is different. Insert the hook into the vertical stitch, and the loop on the hook, yarn over and pull through, repeat this until the end of the row. Now cut the yarn and weave the end into the last row with a yarn needle.

Changing Colors

At the end of a forward row when two loops are on the hook, pull the new color through the two loops and chain 1. Now begin the return row using the new color. Continue making forward and return rows until the pattern changes color again. If the pattern is striped, or color blocked, changing color works best on the forward row.

Pattern and Stitch Abbreviations

To complete a beginner pattern and read it properly, you will need to remember six abbreviations. Pattern instructions vary depending on who created the pattern, but the all patterns use these abbreviations. Advanced stitches have different abbreviations but they are not necessary here. The six abbreviations used in the instructions of a pattern will look similar to this:

> *To begin Ch 15, now Yo and pull through the second stitch from the hook. Yo and pull through each stitch and leave the loop on the hook until there are 15 loops on the hook. *Now Yo and pull through the first stitch, then Yo and pull through the next two stitches. Rep * until 15 rows have been completed. Now finish off the fabric. The finished fabric should be a 15 x 15 square.*

Practice making this square to gain skill in using a pattern and Tunisian crocheting. It is easy once you understand the abbreviations. The finished practice squares can be used to create a granny Afghan. There are no double or treble crochet stitches in Tunisian crochet, some advanced stitches have abbreviations too the beginner projects in this book do not use any advanced techniques.

- Ch – Chain
- Yo – Yarn over

- Sts – Stitches
- Sk – Skip
- Sl St – Slip stitch
- Rep – Repeat
-

All of the beginner patterns in this book use these five abbreviations. Once you know the simple stitches and the abbreviation's you can complete a beginner pattern. With the abbreviations here you can make almost anything, and read beginner patterns. Make a note of these abbreviations on a note card and keep it with your crochet stash. Beginner patterns are easy to read and complete and even easier if you have a cheat sheet handy.

A beginner pattern uses simple stitches but that does not mean it is not a beautiful pattern. Simple items like scarves, washcloths, and wrist warmers are easy to make. Tunisian crochet creates a waffle weave type of fabric that is thick and cushy. Anything made with the simple Tunisian stitch will make a great gift…if you can part with it.

Chapter 2 – Beginner Patterns

All of these patterns use the simple Tunisian stitch, some have color changes, but all of them are created with one easy stitch. Different yarns are best for specific projects, follow the instructions for each pattern, the pattern includes information about what yarns to use. If there is no specific yarn mentioned then it is safe to use regular thickness.

The instructions for each pattern use the abbreviations for Tunisian crochet and include the amount of yarn needed and the approximate size of the finished project. If you are just practicing, any yarn will do, but if you plan to use the item it pays to check out the different yarn brands and blends. Cotton works best for any type of towel or wash cloth because it soaks up water instead of pushing it around the way polyester will.

It is a good idea to find and purchase a set of Afghan hooks in different gauges. The gauge of the hook determines the size of the stitch and the density of the finished fabric. Some patterns do not specify a gauge and other do, either way it is always better to have a choice.

If you plan to create large items you may want to get a set of stitch markers. Stitch markers keep your place when you are making complicated or large items. No one wants to count stitches because they lost count, stitch markers can be used to keep track for you.

As you work through these patterns remember to keep your stitches loose, not too loose that the stitch is sloppy, just loose enough to keep the fabric from curling. Tight stitches cause the fabric to curl up on itself and the hook may get caught as you pull through stitches. The best way to establish how loose is to work a practice piece and adjust the tension until you like the stitch the fabric does not look sloppy.

1 - *Thick and Thirsty Wash Cloth*

You will need one skein of 100% cotton yarn. The finished wash cloth will be an 8in x 8in square. Follow the instructions on the skein for fabric care. Work the stitches loosely so the fabric will not curl up.

To begin, Ch 42 do not turn the work, Yo and pull through the second stitch from the hook. Leave the loop on the hook, *Yo and pull through each stitch and leave each loop on the hook, Rep * until the end of the row, there is now 42 loops on the hook. This is the preparation and foundation row.

Without turning the project, Yo and pull through the second loop on the hook, *Yo and pull through the next two loops on the hook. Rep * until the end of the row. Without turning the work, pick up the first vertical stitch and begin the forward row. Continue making return and forward rows until the fabric has 8 rows then finish off.

2 - *Alternate Patterns for Striped Wash Cloth and a Boarder Wash Cloth*

To make a striped wash cloth, purchase two complimenting colors of cotton yarn, one skein each. Change colors every two return rows. To add a border to a solid color wash cloth, use a contrasting color of yarn and insert the hook into a corner of the wash cloth. Ch 1, and insert the hook into the first chain, Yo and pull through, insert the hook into the same stitch, Yo and pull through, do this four times on each corner. Then insert the hook into the second stitch from the hook, *Yo and pull the yarn through the loop. Continue to Rep * until the border surrounds the wash cloth.

3 - Tunisian Scarf

For this scarf, you will need 7 skeins of yarn any color, and a J gauge Afghan hook. The completed scarf is 12in wide and 72in long.

Ch 42 then insert the hook into the second stitch from the hook, Yo and pull through the stitch and leave the loop on the hook, continue until the end of the row. This is the foundation row and the preparation row.

Now begin the first return row. Insert the hook into the second stitch from the hook, Yo and pull through the loop. *Insert the hook into the next two stitches, Yo and pull through both. Repeat * until the end of the row.

Now begin the forward row. Insert the hook through the first vertical stitch, Yo and pull through, continue until the forward row is complete. Continue making return and forward rows until the fabric is 70in. long. Now finish off, cut the yarn and weave the end into the last row.

4 - Alternate Pattern for a Striped Scarf and a Color Block Scarf

To make this scarf using two colors or more choose and purchase complimenting colors of yarn. Make sure to purchase 7 skeins all together. To make stripes, change colors every two returns. To make color block, change colors every twelve returns.

5 - Striped Pot Holders

You will need two contrasting colors of yarn, one skein of each color. A J Gauge Afghan hook, and a yarn needle. The finished pot holder will be 8in x 8in with a loop for hanging.

Ch 42 then using the same color insert the hook into the second stitch from the hook, Yo and pull the yarn through the stitch, leave the loop on the hook. This is the foundation and preparation row.

Start the first return row with the second color, *complete two rows, one return and one forward, then change colors. Rep * until 8 rows are completed and finish off. Weave the end into the last row using a yarn needle.

To make the loop for hanging, insert the hook into the corner of the fabric and Ch 10. Now insert the hook into the same corner, Yo and pull through. Cut the yarn and weave the end into the last row with a yarn needle.

6 - Two Tone Throw Pillow

This pattern requires two contrasting colors of yarn, one skein of each color. One bag of polyester fill, a J gauge Afghan hook, and a yarn needle. The finished pillow is approximately 12in x 12in. One 12in square will be one color and the other 12in square will be a contrasting color.

Ch 42, then insert the hook into the second stitch from the hook, *Yo and pull through, leave the loop on the hook. Rep * until the row is complete. This is the foundation and preparation rows.

Begin the return row, Ch 1, *Yo and pull through two stitches/loops on the hook. Rep * until only one loop remains on the hook. Begin the forward row, *insert the hook into the next vertical stitch, Yo and pull through, leave a loop on the hook. Rep * until the row is complete then finish off.

Alternate between the return row and the forward row until 12 rows have been completed. Using the contrasting color follow the same instructions and create a 12 in square. Using the yarn needle, sew both squares together leaving a small gap so the pillow can be stuffed. Stuff the pillow then stitch gap closed and the pillow is complete.

7 - Striped Granny Square

The granny square is a great way to use up left over yarn. One skein will make several granny squares. The squares can be used to create scarves, throws, and pillows, just sew the squares together using a yarn needle. This granny square is striped and when complete it is 12in x 12in. Use a J gauge Afghan hook.

Ch 42, then insert the hook into the second stitch from the hook. *Yo and pull through stitch and leave the loop on the hook. Rep * until the row is complete and one loop remains on the hook. This is the foundation and preparation rows.

Change colors and begin the return row, Ch 1, * Yo and pull through the next two loops on the hook, Rep * until the end of the row, leave one loop on the hook. Now begin the forward row, * insert the hook into the next vertical stitch, Yo and pull through leaving a loop on the hook. Rep * until the row is complete.

Continue changing colors every two rows until 12 rows are completed. Finish off and weave the end into the fabric. To create a boarder around the granny square, choose a color and * Ch 1 in any corner of the fabric. In the same stitch, insert the hook and Ch 1 three more times. Now there are four stitches in the corner of the fabric. ** Insert the hook into the next stitch, Yo and pull through both stitches leaving one loop on the hook. Rep ** until the row reaches the next corner, now Rep * and begin the next section. Rep ** until the next corner then Rep*. Continue this until the entire square has a boarder. Finish off and weave the loose end into the fabric with a yarn needle.

8 – Crazy Granny Square Throw

Using pattern 7, the striped granny square, create 15 squares. Each square is 12in x 12in so the finished throw will be 3ft wide and 5ft long. Lay out the granny squares in a pattern. Place one square with the stripes in a horizontal position, the next square with the stripes in a vertical position, and the third square with the stripes in a horizontal position then sew the squares end to end using a yarn needle. Every grouping is three squares across. For the next row, place the first square with the stripes in a vertical position, the next in a horizontal position, and the last one in a vertical position, then sew them end to end using a yarn needle. Alternate between both patterns until all five rows are complete.

Now sew each row to the next until all five rows are sew together one on top of the other. To give the throw a finished look, choose one of the colors in the stripes and begin in a corner. Place four crochet stitches in each corner as the boarder progresses. Crochet using a single crochet stitch around the entire throw.

9 - Warm and Comfy Cowl

To complete this cowl you will need two skeins of yarn any color and a J gauge Afghan hook. This cowl is approximately 15in long. Begin the project with Ch 50, insert the hook into the second stitch from the hook, Yo and pull through leaving one loop on the hook. Continue this until the row is complete. These are the preparation and foundation rows.

To begin the return row, Ch 1 then Yo and pull through the loop. * Yo and pull through two loops on the hook. Rep * until the return row is complete and one loop remains on the hook.

To begin the forward row, * insert the hook into the next vertical stitch, Yo and pull through leaving one loop on the hook. Rep * until the end of the row.

Alternate between the return and forward row until there are 15 rows completed, then finish off the last row. To make sure the fabric lays properly and does not curl, it should be blocked. To block the fabric and remove any curling, use push pins and pin the fabric down on a thick piece of cardboard or cork board. Stretch the fabric where it needs it to create a perfect rectangle. Spray the fabric lightly with warm water and leave it to air dry. When the pins are removed, the fabric will lay flat.

To finish the cowl, sew both ends of the rectangle together using a yarn needle. The finished project is thick, cozy, cowl that defies the worst winter has to offer.

This pattern can be altered to size, just change the original number of Ch stitches in the beginning to reflect the width and the number of rows to reflect the length.

10 -Simple Cozy Wrist Warmers

Wrist warmers are a fun and fashionable way to keep warm while texting. Wrist warmers cover the palms, wrists, and part of the arm but the fingers and thumb are exposed. This pattern requires two skeins of yarn, a J gauge Afghan hook, and a yarn needle. The finished wrist warmers will be 12 in long.

Ch 42 then insert the hook into the second stitch from the hook. Yo and pull through the stitch leaving one loop on the hook. * Insert the hook into the next stitch, Yo and pull through leaving one stitch on the hook. Rep * until the row is complete. These are the foundation and preparation rows.

Ch 1 then Yo and pull the yarn through the stitch, * Yo and pull through the next two stitches. Rep * until the return row is complete and one loop is left on the hook.

*Insert the hook into the next vertical stitch, Yo and pull through leaving a loop on the hook. Rep * until the forward row is complete and one loop is left on the hook.

Alternate between the return and forward rows until the fabric has 12 rows. The fabric is now 12 in long, you can change the width of the wrist warmers for size by adding or deleting rows until the fabric wraps around the wrist and fits snug but not tight.

Finish the warmers by folding the fabric in half and sewing the seam long ways. As the sewing gets closer to the top of the warmer, leave a 2in gap for the thumb. The warmers are now complete but decorative stitching or any other embellishment may be added to personalize the warmers.

Create Your Own Pattern

Once you have learned the simple Tunisian stitch, you can use your new skill to create your own patterns. To create your own pattern you will need count the number of chain stitches you will use, and count the number of rows your project will need.

Begin the pattern with information about the amount of yarn needed, the hook used, any other tools needed and the size of the project. The next step is use the abbreviations to explain how to work your pattern.

Before you create any pattern try it out first to be sure it is what you want it to be. Any pattern you create can be shared with others or just created for yourself. With a little practice and patience you will be able to create patterns and project yourself.

Chapter 3 – Gifting and Selling

Many people crochet items for gift giving. A handmade item such as a scarf or Afghan is always a welcome gift. As you become skilled with the Tunisian crochet stitch you will be able to create everything from sweaters to blankets and shams.

It is always best to make items that do not rely on size when gifting. Creating a sweater that fits is difficult when the individual is not measured for it. Sizing depends on more than just measuring and fitting, it requires perfect stitches so the item will fit properly. Create items like throw blankets, wrist warmers, shawls and hats for winter gift giving. Small items work up quickly with Tunisian crochet and the waffle weave is dense and warmer than traditional crochet or knit.

If you stick with it and learn more advanced stitches and techniques such as the Tunisian lace stitch or goblin stitch, you may be able to make money with your hobby. Many people love crochet items but they do not want to make them, this is where your skill comes in.

Before setting up a web site or listing your items on other internet sites, make sure you have enough items already made. The orders may come in faster than you can make them so maintain several items in stock.

When you begin offering your items for sale be sure you stitch a small tag with your name or company name so individuals know where the item came from. The best way to begin selling is to start small. Sell small items that you can work up quickly if they sell out. Once you have established yourself you can move on to bigger more elaborate projects.

Conclusion

Tunisian crochet is unique, it may look complicated but it is very simple learn. This book has provided all of the skills needed to begin the hobby of Tunisian crochet. Learning more advanced techniques will give all of your crochet projects a polished look but the simple Tunisian stitch is enough to create anything you can imagine.

This new found skill is sure to make you happy when you finish your first handmade scarf or wrist warmers. Make sure you keep enough yarn on hand, nothing is worse than starting a project and having to stop before it is finished because you ran out of yarn. Try different gauge hooks to broaden your skill base and different yarn thickness to personalize the item.

Although everyone has seen those odd long crochet hooks next to the familiar ones in the craft stores, most people do not know how to use them. After reading this book, anyone can use the Afghan hook to work up some warm, cozy, fabric for cold winter nights, or a new trendy cell phone holder.

Tunisian crochet never gets boring. There are always new colors, new patterns, and new skills to choose and learn. It is easy to keep things fresh, just change up the yarn colors or learn a new stitch. Yarn is available in so many textures, thickness, and styles you can use one pattern and create several different looking results.

Blankets and other items will need to be washed and cared for. Information on how to care for each style or brand of yarn is on the yarn packaging. Always follow the yarn manufactures care instructions to keep your items looking their best.

Tunisian crochet works great on large projects and small projects because the stitches are tight and uniform. These stitches work great for items like cat toys, dog toys, and for making all sorts of soft toys for babies and young children. Patterns for toys and other fun stuff are available on line in e-books and on blogs.

Always save the left over yarn, there are always new and exciting projects to tackle with yarn scraps. Scraps are great for granny squares and granny squares are great for blankets. It is a good idea to package up yarn scraps and keep them in a plastic container or bag to keep them clean and ready to use.

Now you have ten items that you can create and enjoy. They may end up finding a new home when birthdays and holidays come around. Once you are hooked it is difficult to stop crocheting. It is ok though, everyone wants something homemade and those projects you completed will find new homes quickly.

Tunisian Crochet Blankets

Introduction

Tunisian crochet, also referred to as afghan crochet, is a little different from traditional crochet, the rows appear similar to the weaving pattern created by knitting. A long crochet hook or flexible afghan hook is used for Tunisian crochet because the technique requires several stitches on the hook like knitting does. Tunisian crochet is an elegant alternative to traditional crochet, it looks different and gives you more choices for making everything from sweaters and scarfs to blankets and throws.

Working with Tunisian crochet is not difficult. The blankets work up quickly and the patterns you can create with Tunisian crochet is just as diverse as traditional crochet. Everything from potholders to baby blankets can be done using Tunisian techniques.

Choose a blanket that matches your skill level and work your way up to the more detailed projects. The required tools for Tunisian crochet are the same as those used for traditional crochet except for one minor difference. A Tunisian crochet hook is much longer than a traditional hook and it has a stopper on the end to keep the stitches on the hook as you work.

Take your time with each project, if you are a beginner, you will gain speed and accuracy as you continue to practice the stitches. You can even modify your project by changing up the colors used for each blanket.

Chapter 1 – How to Tunisian Crochet

Tunisian Crochet works up quicker than traditional crochet and the textile resembles a weave similar to knitting. Tunisian crochet begins the same as traditional crochet, with a chain. The length of the chain depends on the pattern/project. After creating the chain, you insert the afghan hook into the stitch in the chain and pull through, keeping the loop on the hook.

As you move along, you will gather the loops on the afghan hook and when you finish the row, it is time to create the forward pass. After the forward pass you will complete the return pass. This stitch is called the Tunisian simple stitch, follow the images below to learn how to create the Tunisian simple stitch.

The Tunisian simple stitch and the Tunisian knit stitch are used in the patterns in this book, you will use some traditional stitches too. There is a table of abbreviations and the stitches used to help you as you work to complete each blanket.

Tunisian Simple Stitch – Tss/TSS

Insert hook into second stitch from the hook

Yarn over/Yo

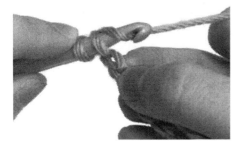

Pull the yarn through one loop on the hook so there is one loop on the hook

Insert the hook into the next stitch

Yo and pull through one loop on the hook now there is one loop on the hook

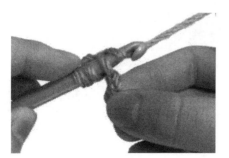

Continue with Yo and pull through first loop on the hook until the number of loops on the hook is the same as the number of stitches used in the original chain

Yo and pull through the first stitch/loop on the hook

Yo and pull through the next two loops on the hook

Continue alternating between one and two loops until the end is reached

One finished row of the Tunisian Simple Stitch

Tunisian Knit Stitch – Tks/TKS

The Tunisian knit stitch differs from the simple stitch because the hook is inserted under the vertical bars or the stitches, not through. Create the first row of Tunisian simple stitch then on each forward pass insert the hook under the vertical stitches, Yo and pull through. The return pass is the same as the return pass in the simple stitch, Yo and pull through the first loop on the hook, then insert the hook Yo and pull through the next two loops on the hook.

Chapter 2 – Crochet Abbreviations

This master list contains all of the abbreviations used in crochet patterns. This list contains traditional stitches as well as special instructions that are expressed with an abbreviation. Tunisian stitches include the Tunisian simple stitch and the Tunisian knit stitch.

Crochet Master List

Abbreviation	Directions	Abbreviation	Directions
[ ]	Complete the instructions inside the brackets the number of times indicated	FPdc	Front post and double crochet
( )	Complete the instructions inside the parentheses the number of times indicated	FPsc	Front post single crochet
*	Repeat the instructions after the asterisk the number of times indicated	FPtc	Front post double crochet
**	Repeat the instructions between the asterisks the number of times indicated	G	Gram
"	Inches	hdc	Half double crochet
Alt	Alternate	inc	Increase
Approx	Approximately	lp	Loop
Beg	Beginning	m	Meter

Bet	Between	MC	Main Color
BL	Back Loop	mm	Millimeter
Bo	Bobble	oz	Ounces
BP	Back Post	p	Pico
BPdc	Back post double crochet	pat	Pattern
BPsc	Back post single crochet	pc	Popcorn
BPtc	Back post treble crochet	pm	Place Marker
CA	Color A	prev	Previous
CB	Color B	rem	Remaining
CC	Coordinating Color	rep	Repeat
ch	Chain Stitch	rnd	Rounds
ch-	Previous chain stitch	RS	Right Side
ch-sp	Chain Space	sc	Single Crochet
CL	Cluster	sc2tog	Single crochet 2 together
cm	Centimeter	sk	Skip
cont	Continue	Slst	Slip stitch
dc	Double Crochet	sp	Space

dc2tog	Double crochet two stitches together	st	Stitch
dec	Decrease	Tch or t-ch	Turn stitch
dtr	Double Treble	tbl	Through the back loop
FL	Front Loop	tog	Together
Foll	Follow	tr	Treble crochet
FP	Front Post	trtr	Triple treble crochet
		WS	Wrong side
		yd	Yard
		yo	Yarn over
		yoh	Yarn over hook
		Tss	Tunisian Simple Stitch
		Tks	Tunisian Knit Stitch

Chapter 3 – Squares, Stripes, and Solids

Textured Tunisian Afghan

Figure 1 (Ravelry, 2015)

This unique blanket uses a combination of the Tss stitch and a triple crochet stitch for the cables. This blanket is done in a solid color; the image shows the blanket done in white but you can choose any color you like.

Tunisian Cable Blanket
(Tunisian Cable Blanket, 2015)

Skill Level: Beginner-Intermediate

- Materials needed: 6 skeins of sport weight yarn any color. The blanket uses two strands held together as one.
- Any size afghan hook, the size determines the size of the stitch and that is up to you with this pattern
- Yarn needle

Finished Size: You can make this blanket any length you want. Just finish and tie off when you are happy with the length.

Pattern
<u>Tc panel and make 3</u>

Row 1: Ch 27

Row 2: Make two rows of Tss

Row 3 Part A: Tss in the 1st three sts. In the 4th st make tc as follows-Yo twice, insert hook in vertical bar two rows below, Yo and pull through 2 loops, Yo and pull through 2 loops, leave 1 loop on the hook. Tss st in next 3 sts, tc in 4th st, repeat across then end with 3 tss.

Row 3 Part B: Tss as 2nd pass

Row 4 Part A: Tss in 1st three sts. In 4th st, make tc st as follows-Yo twice, insert hook in vertical bar two rows below, Yo and pull through 2 loops, Yo and pull through 2 loops and leave 1 look on the hook. Tss in next 3 sts, tc in 4th st, across and end with 3 tc sts.

Row 4 Part B: Tss at 2nd pass

Repeat rows 4A and 4B until desired length is reached and bind off with tss

Make 2 Tss panels as long as the others.

Finishing
Join panels with the wrong sides facing, alternated between the cabled sections and the plain panels. Attach the panels from behind using the loops on the backside of the work.

Minty Squares Tunisian Blanket

This pattern resembles traditional crochet granny squares but the stitch used is the Tunisian Simple Stitch. The colors used for this pattern are listed in the directions but feel free to substitute any colors you like. The pattern uses traditional crochet abbreviations.

Minty Squares Tunisian Blanket
(Red Heart Yarns, 2015)

Skill Level: Beginner-Intermediate

- Materials needed: Red Heart "super-saver" yarn. A) 3 skeins of soft-white, 1 skein each of, B) cornmeal, C) country blue, D) pale plum, E) frosty green and F) light raspberry
- 6.5 Afghan hook
- 6mm crochet hook
- Yarn needle

Finished size: 43" X 60.5"

Pattern
This blanket is created from blocks, similar to the way a granny blanket is created. For this pattern you will need 7 blocks of each color yarn. To begin, use the 6mm crochet hook and ch 16.

Make 2 tss panels the same length as the other panels

Row 1: Keep all loops on the hook. Pull a loop through the second ch in the hook and through each of the ch until you have 16 loops on the hook. Without turning, work back, Yo and pull through 1 loop, Yo and pull through 2 loops, continue until you have removed 15 loops and one loop is left on the hook

Row 2: With the yarn at the back of the work, draw up a loop through the next vertical bar/stitch, *with the yarn in the front of the work, draw up a loop through the next vertical bar*7 times. With the yarn at the back of the work, draw a loop through the last loop, there is now 16 loops on the hook. Work back without turning, *Yo and draw through 1 loop, Yo and draw through 2 loops*15 times.

Row 3: With the yarn at the front of the work, draw up a loop through the next vertical bar/stitch, "with the yarn in back of the work, draw up a loop through the next vertical bar*7 times. With the yarn at the front of the work, draw up a loop through the last loop, there is now 16 loops on the hook. Without turning, Yo and pull through 1 loop, Yo and pull through 2 loops, continue until you have removed 15 loops and one loop is left on the hook.

Row 4-13: Repeat rows 2-3 5 times

Row 14: *With the yarn at the back of the work, draw a loop through the next vertical bar and through the loop on the hook. With the yarn at the front of the work, draw a loop through the next vertical bar and through the loop on the hook* 7 times. With the yarn at the back of the work, draw a loop through the next vertical bar and through the loop on the hook and tie off

One block is now complete. Repeat steps 1 through 14 7 times in each color yarn.

Block Boarders

Round 1: With the right side facing the front, use the 6mm crochet hook and Join color A in the top right hand corner stitch and ch 3. *Skip the next stitch, dc, ch1 dc in the next stitch 6 times. Skip next stitch, dc in last stitch, ch2 and turn to work down the side, dc in first row end, dc, ch1, dc, in the next row end, skip next row end, dc, ch1, dc 5 times skip next row end, dc in next row end, ch 2* Turn and work across lower edge, dc in 1st stitch, repeat *to* one more time, now join with a slip stitch in top of ch 3 then tie off.

Round 2: With the same color as center block, join st in same st as joining, ch1, sc in same stitch. *ch1, sc in next ch – 1 space 6 times. Ch1 skip next dc, sc in next dc, now sc, ch2, sc in the corner ch, 2nd stitch, sc in next dc, ch1, sc in next ch – 1 space 6 times. Ch1, skip next dc, sc in next dc, sc, ch2, sc in the corner ch 2nd stitch*. Sc in next dc, now repeat *to* one more time, now join in first sc and tie off.

Round 3: Join A in top right hand corner, ch-2nd stitch, ch3, dc, ch2, dc2, all in the same stitch. *skip next sc. Dc in next sc, 2dc in next stitch 7 times. Skip next sc, dc in next sc. 2dc, ch2, 2dc, in the 2nd corner stitch. Repeat from * around the block, now join in top of ch3 and tie off.

Assemble the Blanket

B	D	E	F	C
F	C	B	D	E
D	E	F	C	B
C	B	D	E	F
E	F	C	B	D
B	D	E	F	C
F	C	B	D	E

ASSEMBLY DIAGRAM

(Red Heart Yarns, 2015)

Arrange the blocks according to the diagram, using the 6mm crochet hook, join the blocks together from the back, through the back loops using a slip stitch.

Peppermint Twist Afghan

This afghan is simple to do and looks great anytime of year. This pattern is worked with two strands of yarn held together and crocheted as one. The simple afghan stitch and the double yarn makes this a cozy blanket for cold winter nights.

Peppermint Twist Afghan
(Peppermint Twist Afghan, 2015)

Skill Level: Beginner-Intermediate

- Materials needed: Red Heart supersaver or classic or any brand 4-ply worsted. 35oz of cherry red, 28oz of white, and 12oz of paddy green
- 10in size P double ended crochet hook
- Size N traditional crochet hook
- Yarn needle

Finished Size: 51" x 67"

Pattern
Row 1: Using the double crochet hook, ch 23 holding 2 strands of cherry red as one. Insert into 2nd ch from hook and Yo and pull through adding a loop to the hook. *insert hook into next ch, Yo and pull through adding another loop to the hook* until there are 23 loops on the hook. Slide all of the stitches to the other

side of the hook, turn the hook so the loops are on the left side. Leave the cherry red yarn uncut, it will be used later.

Row 2: Hold and use two strands of white yarn as one. Using the white strands, make a slip knot on the left side of the hook and pull the white through the loop on the hook. *Work from left to right and Yo, pull through 2 loops on the hook, one of each color (remember two strands together is one loop)* until there is only one loop left on the hook.

Row 3: Do not turn the work. Work from right to left with the white yarn. Insert the hook into the 2nd stitch from the hook, pull through, leave the loop on the hook, insert the hook through the next vertical bar, Yo and pull through a new loop. *Skip the next vertical bar and insert hook into the next horizontal stitch, Yo and pull through, insert hook under next vertical stitch, Yo and pull through leaving the loop on the hook* Repeat * to* until there are 23 loops on the hook. Slide stitches to other side of hook and leave the yarn uncut.

Row 4: Turn hook and use both strands of cherry red yarn as one. Work from left to right, Yo and pull yarn through first loop on the hook. *Yo and pull through next loop on the hook, now there are 2 loops on the hook* Repeat * to * until 1 loop remains on the hook.

Row 5: Repeat row 3 with cherry red

Row 6: Repeat row 4 with white

Rows 7-144 Repeat rows 3 through 6 then end with a Row 4

Row 145: Work from right to left with cherry red, ch 1 and skip the first vertical bar. * Insert the hook into the top of the next horizontal stitch, Yo and pull through the stitch and the loop on the hook* Repeat * to * until end of row. Tie off the cherry red and cut the white.

Edging
Join two strands of paddy green held together as one to any dc corner with sc. *work 3 scs in each corner dc, (dc in skipped st or row, below next ch – 1 sp, sc in next dc) to next corner* repeat * to * around, end last repeat with slip stitch in beginning sc, tie off.

Add edging to two more strips in the same way, then turn the remaining strips over so the white side is facing and add edging the same way.

Assembly
Face one red side to one white side and whip stitch with the yarn needle through the back loops only using paddy green.

Outer Afghan Edging
Join paddy green using a slip stitch, then use a hdc in each stitch around, finish and join with a slip stitch and tie off.

Finish off the afghan by weaving in any loose yarn with the yarn needle.

Chapter 4 – Baby Blankets and Throws

Baby blankets and throws are smaller than the average afghan or blanket. For beginners it may be easier to crochet a baby blanket or throw because the patterns are shorter and it takes less time to complete.

Most patterns for Tunisian baby blankets and throws use the Tunisian simple stitch and not much else. Although these baby blankets and throws use the Tunisian simple stitch, some also use other techniques for decoration or to add interest to the finished project.

All the patterns in this book are perfect for beginners and intermediate crocheters but that does not mean they are simple looking or boring. The Tunisian stitch itself adds a special character to ordinary blankets that traditional crochet stitches like the single or double crochet do not have.

These patterns are perfect for warming up family member in the living room or cuddling a new baby with warmth and a touch of love. Although some of the patterns have instructions for color, feel free to choose any colors you wish and switch them out with the ones listed. The important part is to make sure you buy the right amount of yarn for each project.

There are differences in yarn, they differ in thickness or strand amount and the thread used for creating the yarn. Some yarns use only natural dyes and natural fibers and yarns like baby yarn is softer and a bit thinner than a wool or wool blend yarn. Choose a yarn that is compatible with the project you are creating and be sure to buy the right number of skeins to finish the project.

Entrelac Baby Blanket

This Entrelac baby blanket has a diamond pattern and solid border. The pattern uses standard abbreviations and the Tunisian simple stitch. The design is in the pattern not the stitch. Learn to crochet with an Entrelac style will add a new skill to your crochet repertoire and you can apply it in your own creations when you begin making your own blankets.

Entrelac may seem daunting for those who are beginners but looks can be deceiving. Unlike some crochet items that use special stitches and techniques to create a beautiful blanket, Entrelac uses only one stitch. Using multiple colors for an Entrelac blanket can resemble a quilt. Using only one color for Entrelac blankets will still give it a distinct look. The alternating squares/diamonds create a textured pattern that is distinct from row to row.

Once you learn the technique of Entrelac you can use it to create anything you want. This style looks great for hats, socks, scarves, pillows…the list goes on.

The Entrelac technique never fails to impress and the finished project looks like you spent forever on it. This is one technique that has been borrowed from knitting that works really well for Tunisian crochet.

Entrelac Baby Blanket Pattern
(McGonigal, 2010)

Skill Level: Beginner-intermediate

- Materials Needed: Two contrasting colors of medium weight yarn, one color for A and one color for B. 500 yards of each color.

- Size 10 Tunisian crochet hook/Afghan hook

- Yarn needle

Pattern
Notes about this pattern

- The return pass is created: *Yo pull through two loops and repeat from * across

- Binding off: Insert the hook from the front to the back between two vertical bars of the stitch then Yo and pull up a loop, then Yo and pull through both loops on the hook

- Picking up loops from the bind off row: Insert the hook through two loops of the bind off chain then Yo and pull up a loop

- M1 means Make one stitch: Insert the hook from the front between the next two vertical bars then Yo and pull up a loop

- Pay attention to the tension you are using, try to keep an even tension while you work, not too tight, not too loose

Begin with Color A and Ch 74

The first tier will have twelve base triangles
Row 1: Insert hook in second St from the hook, Yo and pull up a loop, now there are 2 loops on the hook then return pass

Row 2: M1 then Tks in the next vertical bar. Now insert the hook in the next ch and pull up a loop. There should be 4 loops on the hook, now return pass

Row 3: Tks in the next two vertical bars then M1 between the last vertical bar and the edge of the last row. Insert the hook in the next ch and pull up a loop, now there are 5 loops on the hook, then return pass

Row 4: Tks in the next 3 vertical bars, M1 between the last vertical bar and the edge of the last row. Insert the hook in the next ch and pull up a loop, now there are 6 loops on the hook, then return pass

Row 5: Tks in the next 4 vertical bars, M1 between the last vertical bar and the edge of the last row. Insert the hook in the next ch and pull up a loop, now there are 7 loops on the hook, then return pass

Row 6: Tks in the next 5 vertical bars, M1 between the last vertical bar and the edge of the last row. Insert the hook in the next ch and pull up a loop, now there are 8 loops on the hook, then return pass

Row 7: Bind off 6 stitches. Slst in same ch as the last stitch in the last row. One triangle is now complete

Repeat rows 1-7 11 more times so there are 12 triangles, on the last triangle Slst in the last ch and tie off

Tier A is 1 left triangle, 11 squares, and 1 right triangle

Right-Edge Triangle
Join color B in the bottom corner of the first triangle made or in the last edge of the previous right-edge triangle for successive tiers

Row 1: Ch 2 then pull up a loop in the second ch from the hook in the edge of the last row of the first tier. Now there are 3 loops on the hook, then return pass

Row 2: M1 then Tks in the next vertical bar in the edge of the 2nd row of the first tier, now there are 4 loops on the hook, then return pass

Row 3: M1 then Tks in the next 2 vertical bars and in the edge of the 3rd row of the last tier, now there are 5 loops on the hook, then return pass

Row 4: M1 then Tks in the next 3 vertical bars and in the edge of the 4th row of the last tier, now there are 6 loops on the hook, then return pass

Row 5: M1 then Tks in the next 4 vertical bars and in the edge of the 5th row of the last tier, now there are 7 loops on the hook, then return pass

Row 6: M1 then Tks in the next 5 vertical bars and in the edge of the 6th row of the last tier, now there are 8 loops on the hook, then return pass

Row 7: Bind off 6 stitches then Slst in the next stitch of the last tier

Square
Row 1: Pick up 7 stitches from the edge of the last tier, now there are 8 loops on the hook, then return pass

Rows 2-6: Tks in the next 6 vertical bars and in the edge of the next row of the last tier, now there are 8 loops on the hook, then return pass

Row 7: Bind off 6 stitches then Slst in the next stitch of the last tier

Repeat 1-7 10 more times so there are 11 squares made

Left-Edge Triangle
Row 1: Pick up 7 stitches from the edge of the last tier, now there are 8 loops on the hook, then return pass

Row 2: Tks across, now there are 7 loops on the hook, then return pass

Row 3: Tks across, now there are 6 loops on the hook, then return pass

Row 4: Tks across, now there are 5 loops on the hook, then return pass

Row 5: Tks across, now there are 4 loops on the hook, then return pass

Row 6: Tks across, now there are 3 loops on the hook, then return pass

Row 7: Bind off 1 stitch then tie off the yarn

Tier B has 12 squares
Join color A in the first stitch of the last tier and work 12 squares the same as you did for Tier A

Now repeat tier A and then tier B 8 times, now repeat tier A one last time

Finishing Tier has 12 triangles
Join color A to the first stitch of the last tier

Row 1: Pick up 7 stitches from the edge of the last tier, now there are 8 loops on the hook, then return pass

Row 2: Skip the next vertical bar and Tks in the next 5 vertical bars and in the edge of the next row of the last tier, now there are 7 loops on the hook, then return pass

Row 3: Skip the next vertical bar and Tks in the next 4 vertical bars and in the edge of the next row of the last tier, now there are 6 loops on the hook, then return pass

Row 4: Skip the next vertical bar and Tks in the next 3 vertical bars and in the edge of the next row of the last tier, now there are 5 loops on the hook, then return pass

Row 5: Skip the next vertical bar and Tks in the next 2 vertical bars and in the edge of the next row of the last tier, now there are 4 loops on the hook, then return pass

Row 6: Skip the next vertical bar and Tks in the next vertical bar and in the edge of the next row of the last tier, now there are 3 loops on the hook, then return pass

Row 7: Skip the next vertical bar and Slst in the next stitch of the last tier, one triangle is now complete

Repeat rows 1-7 11 more times until there are 12 triangles then fasten off the end

Block the blanket

Weave in all loose ends

(McGonigal, 2010)

Striped Afghan Throw

This pretty afghan can be used as a throw or baby blanket. To make it a throw blanket use a heavier yarn, for a baby blanket use baby yarn for a super soft touch. Use any colors you like for the stripes just follow the instructions for how much you need of each color to complete the throw.

Striped Afghan Throw Pattern
(Gerber, 2015)

Skill Level: Beginner/Easy

- Materials needed: Patons SWS, 110 yards of each color: A) Natural Earth B) Natural Russet and C) Natural Charcoal.
- Size L traditional crochet hook
- Size N Afghan hook
- Yarn needle

Finished Size: 36" x 56"

Pattern
As you finish each row, you will have the previous strand of color waiting, pick up the new color and continue.

This pattern uses the Tss exclusively, for a refresher on the Tss stitch review the stitches in chapter 1.

Color Sequence/Pattern

1: Ch 108 with color A

2: Forward pass, continue with color A

3: Return pass, drop color A and add color B

4: Forward pass, drop color B and add color C

Repeat 2-4 until you have reached your desired length or 56"

Create the finishing row using slip stitches using the traditional crochet hook

Tunisian Lap Blanket

Tunisian Lap Blanket Pattern
(Ravelry, 2015)

Skill Level: Beginner/Easy

- Materials needed: Two colors of yarn, yarn A) 2 skeins, each 104 yards

   Yarn B) 2 skeins, each 104 yards

- Afghan hook size 1
- Yarn needle

Finished Size: 26" x 14"

Pattern
Ch 62 for beginning row

Using only the Tunisian simple stitch/Tss, work 78 rows. Alternate between color A and color B. Use color A on the forward passes and use color B on the return pass. After each pass, leave one color and pick up the next color, do not cut the yarn, leave it until you return to pick it up.

After the last return row, bind off with slip stitches.

Tunisian Afghan in the Round

Tunisian Afghan in the Round
(Reed, 2015)

Skill Level: Easy-Beginner

- Materials needed: Worsted weight yarn in two colors, one for color A and one for color B. Three skeins of each color.
- Size 10.5 double ended Tunisian crochet hook
- Yarn needle

Finished Size: As large or small as you like, continue or end when you decide it is large enough.

Pattern
Color A will always be worked with the right side facing you and color B will always be worked with the wrong side facing you.

<u>Corner Increase is done as follows</u>: Tss into the stitch, Yo and Tss into the stitch again, this creates 3 stitches in 1.

Using color A, ch 4

Round 1: In 4th ch from hook, 2 dc, ch 1, *3 dc, ch 1* repeat * to * 2 times. Join with a slst in top of ch 3. 12 dc, 4 ch in 1 space.

Round 2: Keep the first loop on the hook. *Insert hook into next dc, Yo and pull through* repeat * to * one time. Insert hook into ch 1 space, Yo and pull through.

Yo and insert into ch 1 space again, Yo and pull through, now there are 6 loops on the hook.

Turn the work and push the work to other side of hook. Using color B return pass on the back side of the work by Yo and pull through 1st loop, then Yo and pull through 2 loops and repeat until 2 loops remain on the hook.

*Turn and push work to the other side. Using color A, pick up the loops in each dc. Insert hook in ch 1 space, Yo and pull through, now Yo and insert hook in ch 1 space again, Yo and pull through.

Turn work and push to other side. Using color B, return pass by Yo and pull through 2 loops on the hook, repeat until 2 loops remain on the hook.*

Repeat from * to * 2 more times. Do not join at end of round. 24 stitches

Conclusion

Hopefully this book has inspired you to learn a new type of crochet and use it to create your own creations. Tunisian crochet has many similarities to knitting, the stitches are close and thick make Tunisian crochet a great choice for blankets and other apparel items that need to keep the recipient warm and cozy.

Tunisian crochet seems daunting and intimidating when you firs take a look at it but the truth is, this is just as easy, maybe even easier than traditional crochet. Tunisian offers more versatility than other tricks.

Tunisian uses a tight woven type of material that is suited for situations that arise. It originally started as a knit stitch but crocheters adopted the style for its good looks and thickness. After learning the basics in this book you will have the ability to complete all 7 patterns and show off your new found skills, who knows maybe you will create a family heirloom that will be passed down through your family for ages.

Tunisian Crochet Patterns

Introduction

The Tunisian crochet stitch is known by a few names: The Afghan join, Hook, Railroad Knitting, Shepherd's sewing, weaving, and tricot sew.

Unless you have a customary Tunisian crochet hook, which is a long handed sew snare, then Tunisian sew is truly reasonable for making littler things, for example, wallets, headbands, belts, and other little things which don't require more than twelve join over the column. That is on account of the considerable number of lines keep focused snare, and any more than that, they will tumble off the back end of the snare!

Tunisian Crochet has a long, however discontinuous history; which is the one reasons why it isn't too referred to and famous as weaving and exemplary sew. Most students of history trust that shepherds in the fields made this kind of embroidery, however nobody has discovered surviving confirmation to plainly characterize "when" it was made. The principal "current" appearance of Tunisian Crochet is amid the Victorian Era when distributers started to tap the embroidery market. Lamentably, everybody was calling it something other than what's expected: every distributer had their picked name for the embroidery and they each had their own particular picked line titles. Towards the end of the nineteenth century, even topographical territories had an alternate name for this style of embroidery. The French are credited for calling it Tunisian Crochet, despite the fact that there is no proof to recommend it was begun in Tunis. I haven't discovered the accurate date when Americans started calling it the Afghan Stitch, however the new name was settled by the 1930's.

Tunisian Crochet was well known for the Victorian Era, however for obscure reasons that prominence melted away in the early party of the twentieth Century. There is confirmation of a resurgence of Tunisian Crochet in the late 1960's through the mid 1970's; on the other hand beginning in the mid to late 1980's. After that, Tunisian Crochet has gained enduring ground towards accomplishing the same ubiquity as sewing and exemplary knit. One component keeping Tunisian Crochet down is the fear of distributers to purchase more intricate undertaking examples that utilization Tunisian Crochet; that is evolving... day by day.

Today's fashioners appear to have some kind of uneasy indecision towards Tunisian Crochet. What to call the style of embroidery; what to call the join utilized; how to compose fasten documentations and headings for forming. Previously, these were genuine concerns; in any case, it has been my experience that today's Tunisian Crochet Enthusiast is usual to the perplexity. They know not all the line directions to plainly recognize the mechanics for every line utilized in any case what title the distributer connects to the join.

Chapter 1 – Start with Tunisian Simple Stitch

Tunisian crochet makes a tight fix of woven yarn. It helps in the event that you as of now have a moderate level of solace with standard stitch before leaving on this procedure, however broad sew information is a bit much. The most imperative thing to learn is the Tunisian basic join, yet there are different methods, similar to the Tunisian twofold knit, that can likewise prove to be useful.

Design a Foundation Chain

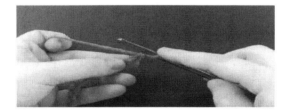

- Join the yarn to your snare utilizing a slipknot, then work an establishment of 10 standard chain lines.
- You can change this number of chains as indicated by your needs. This illustration utilizes 10 chain join, however you ought to modify this number in view of your design's directions or on the fancied length of your work.

Make a Slip Knot

- Make a loop or circle, passing the last part of the yarn underneath the appended side.

- Push the appended side of the yarn up through the circle's base, making a second circle all the while. Fix the first circle around it.

- Embed your knit guide into the second circle. Pull on the last part of the yarn to fix the second circle onto the snare and finish the bunch.

Make a Chain Stitch

- Yarn over the snare's tip once.

- Pull this yarn-over through the circle as of now on your snare. This finishes one chain fasten.

Insert the hook into the second chain from the hook

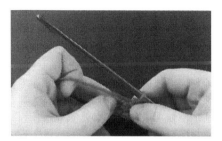

- Yarn over the snare once, then force a circle back through to the front of your piece.

- You can either work your lines into the back circles of your establishment chain or into both the front and back circles. Regardless of which system you utilize, on the other hand, you ought to keep on utilizing the same technique all through the whole work.

- Toward the end of this stride, you ought to have two circles on your snare.

- Note that you are starting your first forward pass. You are additionally making a planning line for whatever is left of your work.

Repeat with the Chain

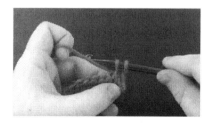

- Take after the same method to draw up a circle through every chain. Proceed until you achieve the end of your establishment chain.

- For every chain, embed the guide into the chain, yarn over the tip, and step the circle back through to the front of the stitch.

- Before the end of this procedure, you ought to have the same number of circles on your snare as you had fastens in your establishment chain. For this case, you will have 10 circles.

- This finishes your first forward pass.

Start Return Pass

- Yarn over the snare's tip, then force this yarn over through one circle on your snare.

- You ought to still have the same number of circles on your snare as some time recently. For this case, you will have 10 circles.

- This is the first fasten in your arrival pass. The rest are comparative, however, not exactly like it.

- Work a second return pass. Yarn over the snare's tip once more. This time, pull the yarn-over through two circles on your snare.

- After this stride, you will have one less circle on your snare. For this sample, you must have nine circles.

Repeat in Reverse

- Repeat the past stride until you achieve the starting point of your work and just have on circle left on your snare.

- For every join, you ought to yarn over the snare and draw the yarn-over through two circles already on the snare.

- Toward the end of every stitch, you will be left with one less circle on your snare.

- Try not to pull through the keep going circle on your snare.

- This stride finishes your first turn around pass. It likewise finishes your preparation row.

- Forward like before. To begin another line of Tunisian knit utilizing the basic join, you should work another forward go in the same fundamental way as the first.

- For this forward pass, embed the snare from right to left into the second vertical bar from the snare. Try not to embed the guide into the vertical bar specifically beneath it; you must utilize the second vertical bar.

- Yarn over the snare's tip and draw it back through to the vertical's front bar. You ought to have two circles on your snare.

- Insert the hook into the next bar, yarn over, and pull it through, giving you three circles on your snare.

- Repeat it, until you have come to the last vertical bar. Try not to work a line into the last vertical bar yet.

Insert the hook into the last two lines of the column

- Find the even bar straightforwardly right of the last vertical bar. After that insert the hook under this flat bar, and also the last vertical bar. Yarn over and pull a circle back through these two fastens to finish your forward pass.

- Note that this stride is just discretionary. On the off chance that coveted, you can essentially draw a circle up from underneath the vertical bar just and reject the flat bar. Utilizing both add soundness to your work, in any case.

- Toward the end of this step, you ought to have 10 circles on your snare, or numerous circles as you had in the foundation chain.

Return Pass

- Complete another return pass line in the same route as the first.
- Yarn over the tip of the snare. Pull this yarn-over through one circle already on the hook.
- Yarn over the snare once more, yet this time, pull it through two circles on your snare. This ought to diminish the quantity of circles on the hook by one. Rehash this progression over whatever remains of the column until there is stand out circle left on the hook.

Repeat the process

- Substitute forward and backward between forward pass and turn around pass columns, finishing at the determination of a converse pass line, until you achieve the end of your straightforward line segment or the end of your general work.
- You can make a whole work utilizing only the Tunisian basic line. You could likewise join the straightforward fasten with different strategies, however, similar to the Tunisian twofold knit.

- On the off chance that you wish to end with just the Tunisian basic line, skip down to the area on completing the Work.

Chapter 2 – Easy Steps of Tunisian Double Crochet

Now, it's time to learn Tunisian double crochet. Follow the following easy to follow steps:

Make a foundation row using Tunisian simple stitch

- The Tunisian twofold sew begins after you have finished an arrangement line utilizing the Tunisian simple line.
- You can work the Tunisian twofold sew into bigger bit of Tunisian basic fastens. The arrangement line is a base begin, yet not a most extreme begin.
- Verify that you have finished an opposite go before you begin the Tunisian twofold sew. There need to just be one circle on your hook when you begin.

Chain two

- Work two standard chain fastens from the circle on your snare.
- These chain fastens will suit the height of Tunisian double crochet row.

Forward pass into the next vertical bar

- Yarn over your hook again, then insert it into the second vertical bar. Yarn over once more, then step this yarn-over back through to the front of your work, making a circle. Yarn over again, then draw your last yarn-over through two circles on the hook.
- Note that the first vertical bar needs to be skirted, as finished with the basic join.

- Leave the last circle of the line on your snare. There ought to as of now be one circle on your snare from before that, then again, giving you a sum of two circles on the snare toward the end of this first double stitch.

- The contrast between the Tunisian simple stitch as well as the Tunisian twofold knit lies completely in this forward pass some portion of the procedure.

Work across the row

- Repeat the past step, working into every vertical stitch of the past until you achieve the end of that past column.

- For each stitch, yarn over the hook, after that insert it into the following vertical bar, and yarn over once more. Move the yarn-over back through to the front, yarn over once more, and draw this last yarn-over through two circles on your snare.

- For the last vertical bar, embed the guide into the level line misleading the privilege of the vertical bar and additionally the vertical bar itself. At the point when pulling a circle back through to the front of the work, verify that you pull it through both bars once more. This adds steadiness to the edge of the work.

- When you achieve the end of your forward pass column, you ought to have 10 circles on your snare, or the quantity of join you began with in your establishment chain.

Reverse pass through stitch

- Yarn over the tip of the snare and draw that yarn-over through one circle beforehand on your stitch.
- Note that the pass go for the Tunisian twofold sew is precisely the same the opposite go for the Tunisian basic fasten.
- Converse go through whatever is left of the line of course. Yarn over the snare, then draw that yarn over through two circles on the stitch.
- You need to be left with one less circle on your hook toward the end of the stitch.
- Repeat this step until one and only circle stays on your hook.

Repeat the process

- Exchange forward and backward between the forward pass and switch go until you achieve the end of your Tunisian twofold sew area or the end of your role in general.
- Continuously end with the decision of a reverse pass.
- Skip down to the area on "Completing the Work" in the event that you are prepared to tie off the work toward the culmination of this step.
-

Chapter 3 – Popular Tunisian Crochet Patters for Men

Man crafts are dependably enjoyable to make, yet can in some cases be hard to discover. Female sew examples are anything but difficult to discover; there's ribbon, laces, and blooms all around you look. In any case, sew is not only for young ladies! Trust it or not, folks acknowledge hand crafted knitted examples, as well.

Sew designs for men can be difficult to find and that is the reason we've gathered our most loved free examples all in one spot for you to appreciate. Every one of these examples would make an amazing natively constructed present thought for any uncommon event including birthdays, commemorations, occasions, and Father's Day. You'll discover examples for men and young men of all ages including babies, youngsters, and grown-ups.

#Pattern 1: Little Man Scarf

The strong shades of this exemplary striped scarf example makes this the perfect example for men and young men of any age. Red and blue are average boyish hues that you can't turn out badly with; even children will appreciate wearing this custom made scarf. You could likewise tweak the look of this scarf by utilizing two of his most loved hues. Utilize the shades of his most loved games group or pick his secondary school or school hues for an example he can wear to football games. It's an immortal plan that will never go out of style.

#Pattern 2: Da Beard Hat

You don't need to waste time at the shopping center scanning for the ideal custom made blessing thought for him; this exceptional knit cap example is certain to be a hit! It's a particular outline that he will totally cherish. This free sew example is a definitive grand slam of man specialties. It's intended to keep his head warm, as well as his face also. He will need to wear when he goes to football games, while he's scooping snow, and notwithstanding when he's just running errands around town.

#Pattern 3: Sports Lapghan

If your child, beau, spouse, or father is a self-broadcasted "games gentleman," then he's going to cherish this free knit afghan design. This sewed afghan is one of the best free examples to stitch for men in light of the fact that you can totally modify it to coordinate his most loved group. Besides, it's fast to work up so it makes an awesome a minute ago blessing thought. Offer this to him for his birthday, Christmas, Father's Day, or on the grounds that.

#Pattern 4: Manly Ripple Afghan

The red and dark shades of this free stitch afghan example makes this the ideal example for any man hollow. Swell afghans are a simple and engaging outline component to make and look incredible in any house. It's an extraordinary cover for him to utilize in the event that he gets icy sitting in front of the TV or playing computer games.

Straightforward Sweater for Him: This is an ageless sweater will be an incredible expansion to any man's closet. The basic style of this fantastic team neck sweater makes this an awesome alternative for all intents and purposes any event including birthdays, occasions, or simply regular wear. Utilize any shading tweed yarn that you think he may like best.

#Pattern 5: Al's Dickey

If your gentleman isn't an immense fanatic of scarves or massive winter sweaters, this free knit example is an incredible choice. It's basically a rectangular piece that is worn around your neck to keep icy air from blowing specifically down his shirt. This is a brisk and simple example to finish and it would make an incredible a minute ago blessing thought for the Christmas season. This dickey is a standout amongst the most flexible free examples to knit for men that you can discover. Indeed, you could even sew one for yourself; then both of you could be twins! Not all man specialties are entirely for men just.

Chapter 4 – Popular Baby Cocoon Tunisian Patterns

Did you realize that a considerable measure of infants touch base amid the month of September? Couples have a good time more around the merry Christmas like Christmas and New Year's, henceforth the September notoriety of child of landings. Other well known months are June, July and August. Numerous individuals appreciate having summer babies so they can arrange birthday parties outside and appreciate the warm climate. With hopeful folks come child showers!

We have assembled a spectacular accumulation of case examples only for you! Figure out how to stitch a percentage of the cutest and most surprising examples.

#Pattern 6: Crochet Cocoon

At the point when child is first conceived, you need to keep all of him pleasant and warm, including the most essential part, his head. These sets make extraordinary child shower blessings to give. The Crochet Cocoon, Hat and Booties set (appeared) is one that every single new mother will simply love. The knit cap and sew booties will keep the infant decent and warm when he's alert, however then you can swaddle him in his new cover for snooze time. Infants need a considerable measure of things in the initial couple of months, so why not run with a set?

#Pattern 7: Baby Cocoon Animal

Have you seen a case for child that resembles a creature? These free examples are so slick and genuinely new since I haven't seen them around much, yet. The Owl Baby Cocoon (appeared) is one of the cutest plans ever. This charming little owl is worked in rounds verifying that toward the end of each round it is slip sewed shut all through the whole stitch design. What's awesome about these child knit examples is that you can pick any hues you wish. On the off chance that you don't have a clue about the sexual orientation of the infant then unbiased hues like green and yellow are the best approach. Something else, this Owl Cocoon would look awesome in either pink or blue. You can even modify the look and add somewhat more flare to the cap and add pom poms to the little ears for a fun look.

#Pattern 8: Unexpected Baby Cocoon

What's your most loved thing to stitch for child? In the event that we haven't persuaded you to make one of these super charming covers yet, then simply hold up a touch longer to see what's in store for you next. Expect the surprising with regards to planning your own particular examples. This fantastic Mermaid Cocoon (appeared) is one of my top choices. Dress your infant young lady in this flawless example and even utilize it as a photography prop for her first photographs. How would you stitch something like this? All things considered, this example is worked in rounds utilizing the half twofold knit join and the back post single sew fasten. Every piece is worked independently while the mermaid top and tiara are really worked in columns!

Chapter 5 – Popular Crochet Fun Patterns

Can you trust we at last endured the icy winter months? In spite of the fact that this winter wasn't exceptionally chilly, at any rate in the Chicagoland region, despite everything I anticipate the hotter climate every season. Furthermore, with that warm climate comes all the really bright things in life, as butterflies and blossoms. Snatch a snare and some brilliantly hued yarn and make some stitch blossom designs. How about we have some butterfly stitch fun, too with this DIY eBook. Download this astonishing spring eBook today and figure out how to knit blooms and butterflies. Knit butterfly examples can be so much fun, particularly on the off chance that you work with various hues or even a variegated yarn.

#Pattern 9: Crochet Flower Pattern

Crochet blossom examples are one of my most loved things to sew at whatever time of year. While you're packaged up beside the chimney you can work up any free knit blossoms to include as extras for your winter gear. Make a little flower example to adorn a cap or even a coat. When you figure out how to knit blooms you can basically make any kind of blossom you wish. The perfect thing about spring is that you can improve your home with free stitch bloom examples and even butterfly sew designs. Rather than purchasing a bunch of blooms you can sew your own. The Double Flowers are anything but difficult to stitch, as well as you can transform them into a delightful strand of festoon to light up your home. Free knit bloom examples like these are fun in light of the fact that you can utilize numerous stitch hues to make your strand.

#Pattern 10: Crochet Buttery

You'll truly adore the butterfly stitch design on page 18. The Flutter By Butterfly Dishcloth is so flawless. It has a tad bit of that 3D look to it, while it's still practical as a dishcloth. I for one wouldn't utilize this butterfly sew design as a dishcloth. I would attempt to get imaginative with it and use it as a fun embellishment. In the event that utilized with light pastel hues I think these would look charming swinging from the roof of a tyke's room. Another thought you can utilize this outline for is a table enhancement. Fold up the wings a smidgen so they can seem, by all accounts, to be taking off the table. This is an extraordinary sample of level knit butterflies, yet there are likewise the amigurumi designs. Huge amounts of butterfly stitch fun can be had with 3D butterflies or 1D.

Chapter 6 – DIY Crochet Blanket Patterns

At the point when the winter season hits, the first things I snatch for are my stitched covers. What's more, when the late spring season hits, unfortunately, the first things I get for are my sewn covers, yet just when the cooling is impacting. Do you see a typical subject here? I adore wrapping myself from head to toe in delicate yarns, so when I see knit cover examples for learners, I hop on them like there's no tomorrow. When I initially figured out how to stitch a sweeping I utilized worsted weight yarns as a part of three sew hues regardless I utilize them right up 'til the present time.

#Pattern 11: Blanket for Kids

Birthdays showers are incredible reasons to sew a cover for a tot. These souvenirs can bring numerous recollections for the little child accepting such a brilliant blessing. In spite of the fact that children don't generally understand the significance of things until they're more established, they'll most likely welcome it over the long haul.

#Pattern 12: Crocheted Throws

It can be not the same as different afghans in light of the fact that they have more brightening examples and are some of the time shorter than covers you use to twist up in. In the event that you simply need somewhat additional solace and style in your home, however, work up one of these extraordinary sew tosses for tenderfoots.

Chapter 7: DIY Crochet Bag Patterns

In case you're searching for something extravagant for a decent event then you'll cherish the decisions of grasps that we have, yet in the event that you're searching for a regular sack then we have recently the thing, as well. We're giving the knit sack designs, you should do nothing more than get your yarn and snares and have at it.

#Pattern 13: The Mesmerizing Messenger Bag

It is genuinely astounding! Knit pack examples like this are celebrated in the sew hues that you pick, yet the example itself is simply staggering. This carefully assembled sack is trendy and spacious and can hold every one of your assets. A pleasant included touch is the discretionary strap agent, so make certain you look at this one!

#Pattern 14: The Pretty Purple Purse

It is worked in a rich purple shading to pass on for. This is a lovely sack design that you can treat yourself with. It's an easygoing looking sack that uses the puff fasten giving it that pleasant surface. The strap is sufficiently long to be worn as a cross-body sack. In case you're searching for effortlessness, then this is your go-to.

#Pattern 15: The Crochet Clutch

It is an adorable knit plan on the grounds that you can adorn it with pretty much anything. This specific DIY grip pack is adorned with two catches, however you can likewise include blossoms, sequins or appliques. This is a basic knit design that can be worked up rapidly in single stitch; the example comprises of just 32 columns.

Conclusion

Since you know how to make crochet patterns you can simply ahead and make every last one in this eBook. Rather than purchasing so as to flush cash down the can a Tory Burch, a Coach or a Fendi tote, sew your own! These outlines are choice and in the event that you make one yourself, it'll be a great deal more incredible. In case you're made a beeline for the workplace, to a wedding or to an outside occasion, we have quite recently the patterns for you.

Tunisian Crochet Projects For Kids

Introduction

Tunisian crochet, also known as Afghan crochet, is a little bit different from your regular crochet. It still has a lot of the basics; you use hooks and yarn to create things from patterns. But there are also some differences that make Tunisian crochet much easier to pick up and learn. Let's get started with a quick look at some of those differences.

Chapter 1 – The Differences Between Tunisian and Regular Crochet

If you've taken a look at crocheting you've probably written it off as something complicated and time consuming to learn. While that's not entirely true it is hard to look past the intimidating nature. Crochet patterns don't make any sense at all unless you know what you're doing. That's also kind of true for Tunisian crochet.

You'll still be dealing with patterns that you have to understand. But you can still get into Tunisian crochet more easily than you could crocheting thanks to the differences between the two.

One of the key differences is the size of the hook. Tunisian crochet is a sort of blend between crocheting and knitting. Though you don't need to know how to knit before you go into Tunisian crochet. What is meant by this is that the hook is longer than the hook in regular crochet. It actually looks a bit like a knitting needle with a hook on the end for crocheting.

Another difference, and the key one that makes it easier to learn Tunisian crochet, is the number of different stitches in a pattern. In regular crocheting there are lots of different stitches. There's the stitch, the double stitch, the treble stitch, the half double stitch, and the list goes on. You also have to turn over every so often. The really difficult things are so difficult because you have to know how to do everything before going into them. This isn't the case with Tunisian crochet.

Tunisian crochet only has five different things to remember. There's the regular chain stitch (characterized in patterns as ch), yarning over (YO), stitches (Sts), skipping (sk), and the slip stitch (Sl St), no double or treble stitches or anything inbetween. Crocheting has so many acronyms and stitches you need a glossary to keep up with them all.

The final major difference between the two is that there is no need to turn your work with Tunisian crochet. One row of Tunisian crochet is made up of two parts. There is the forward pass, which is where you pick up stitches onto the hook, and the reverse pass. The reverse pass is where you work them off the hook. These two bits go together to eliminate the need for turning over as long as you keep the right side of the yarn facing you. A pattern will usually write both passes as one row. Some other patterns won't. So always double check your pattern to make sure you understand it properly.

Those are the three major differences that make this kind of crocheting easier. It does limit what you can do however. Regular crocheting can be used to make all kinds of things but Tunisian crochet needs to be focused around smaller projects. You can make some bigger things but they take longer and are more complicated. This guide is going to focus on the small and easier things. With that said let's take a little deeper look at Tunisian crochet.

Chapter 2 – Getting Started With Tunisian Crochet

If you've worked with crocheting, or know the basics, you'll have an easier time picking up Tunisian crochet. Crocheting begins with a foundation chain and so does Tunisian crochet. With the Tunisian version you need to make a whole foundation row with a forward and return pass. The foundation row is almost always the same style too no matter what pattern or stich you use. It's all about what you do after that basic stitch.

To get started with Tunisian crochet you need to start with a slip knot and a chain stitch. To practice working your basic foundation row make a chain stitch of fifteen chains and go from there. The chain needs to be the same length as the amount of stitches you're going to work with. For example if you're working with ten stitches then your chain needs to be ten chains long. Fifteen is a basic and easy number to work with so use that as your practice.

To start working with your foundation row and working the forward pass start by inserting your hook into the second chain from the hook. That's how things work in regular crocheting too. You almost always ignore the first chain from the hook.

After inserting the hook into the chain you yarn over, which is pulling the yarn over the hook, and then pull up the loop you've made. After that you should have two loops on your hook. You need to keep the loops on the hook at all times. You also need to repeat this step for every chain on the hook. So by the time that you've finished you should have fifteen loops on your hook. That's another major difference between crochet and Tunisian crochet. You keep the loops on the hook. That's why the Tunisian crochet hook is so much longer.

Now it's time to work on the return pass of your foundation row. The return pass goes from left to right. Remember to not turn your work. You're doing this so that you don't have to turn anything over. To start the return pass begin by yarning over, and then pull through the first loop. Then you yarn over again and this time pull through two loops. This is the process you repeat for the rest of the row. You go through two loops at a time for the return pass and stop when you have one loop left. That's your first foundation row down!

This is when you start the first row. What you're working on now is actually a very basic swatch pattern that has you repeat the first row. So when you're done with this row just repeat it until you're satisfied.

Row one has vertical bars that are created from the foundation row. Remember to count them to make sure that you have the same number of bars as you do stitches. You also need to remember to use the last bar at the end.

To start the first rows forward pass skip the first vertical bar and insert your hook into the second one. Yarn over and pull up a loop to get two loops on your hook. Keep up that pattern until you go through every bar and have fifteen loops on your hook.

Now it's time to work the return pass. Yarn over and pull through the first loop. You'll only pull through the first loop at the beginning of the return pass. Then you yarn over and pull through two loops. Keep doing that until you have only one loop left, as you did before. Then you have another fifteen vertical bars. Just keep doing that until you're happy with the size of the swatch.

There's one very simple pattern down and one crucial skill learned. Let's now take a look at some others.

Chapter 3 – Advanced Techniques

As easy as Tunisian crochet is it isn't all just simple stitches and foundation rows. There are other things you need to know. One skill you definitely need to know is how to finish your work when you're done.

When the time comes to finish your work you start by completing the return pass on the last row of the pattern. You can fasten off similar to what you do in regular crochet, which is tightening everything up and then cutting the yarn, or you can do something fun by making a neater edge using slip stitches. To make a neater edge insert the hook under second vertical strand, bypassing the outside edge.

Pull the yarn through both loops of the hook and repeat that action along the row and you'll have made a neat little slip stitch to give your product a more polished look. It looks a lot better than just fastening off and makes the pattern a little more unique.

Another little advanced trick to know how to do is switching colors. Changing the color is needed in some patterns. You can also use it on a single color pattern to add some stripes for a bit of colorful flair. You can also use this technique to switch yarn if you find yourself running out. Whether you want to change colors or switch to a different ball of yarn here is the technique for how to do it.

If you're changing color to create solid stripes in your pattern then you need to change for the start of the forward pass. That means you pick up the new color at the end of the last reverse pass. Just hook in the new color at the end, as you would do with regular crochet. Fit it through the loop and you'll have yourself two solid blocks of color. That's also how you swap yarn of the same color. You'll have two solid blocks of the same color so no one will be able to tell that you switched yarn.

There's another little trick you can do when it comes to swapping colors. You could create two solid blocks of color, and there's nothing wrong with that, but what if you wanted to do something a little more? If you change color at the beginning of the reverse pass, rather than the end, you get an entirely different effect. All you have to do is work the forward pass in the old color, then pick up your new color at the start of the chain in the reverse pass. This makes the old color sort of fold over the new color and create an almost tunnel like effect that helps avoid some issues with the way the color stripes look, as well as adding a unique flair to your project.

There plenty of other little things you can do to add some fun to your project. There's one last one that we'll look at before moving on to some patterns for you to try. The last little advanced thing to show you is how to make a cross stitch.

Begin by chaining an odd number of chains for your foundation row. We recommend seventeen but any odd number will do. You might want to stick to the basic fifteen you've been doing until now. Remember the foundation row will almost always be the same so you don't need us to tell you how to do that again.

To start with the cross stitch skip the first and second vertical bars of your forward pass and instead insert the hook into the third bar. Then you yarn over and pull up a loop, giving you two loops on your hook.

Now, and this is where it gets a little complicated, you need to work into the second bar that you just skipped. That's why you skipped it. There's no need to turn your work or do anything fancy. Just bring the hook back and insert it into the second bar. Yarn over and pull up a loop, giving you three loops on your hook. You should be able to see already that you've made an ever so tiny cross stitch.

You just need to do that all the way across, like you did for the basic stitch. Remember to skip one bar and work on the one after, and then go back through the bar you skipped. That gets the stitches to cross over.

Now it's time to work the return pass. Work from left to right, as you always do on the return, and yarn over and pull through the first loop on the hook. For the rest of the pass you yarn over and pull through two loops, as you did before. Then you just repeat row one until you get the amount of rows you need. After a few rows you'll be able to really see the cross pattern and how great it looks.

Now that you know the basics of how to do Tunisian crochet it's time to take a look at some actual patterns for you to try at home. We're focusing on kid friendly ones. You might even want to teach your kids how to do some Tunisian crochet to give them a hobby. The length of the hooks might make it a little tricky for a small child to pick up but they can definitely give it a good go with a little help.

Chapter 4 – Basic Patterns

In the interests of making things a little easier for you the patterns will be written out properly. It's important to learn how to read them properly when you look online or in magazines for patterns of your own. If you know how to read crochet patterns then you'll know how to read Tunisian ones. If you don't then it's all about the acronyms. It was already shown earlier how the different stitches are written out in a pattern. A regular pattern uses those acronyms and numbers to condense what you have to do into a few lines.

Before you proceed there are two more techniques for you to know. The Tunisian Knot Stitch (TKS) and the Tunisian Full Stitch (TFS). The Knot Stitch is done by skipping the first loop to start with. You might notice that the vertical bars in your pattern go up into the horizontal bars, then back down the other side. To do the Knot Stitch you insert your hook between these two vertical bars under the chain. Then you yarn over and pull a loop.

The Full Stitch is pretty similar in that you skip a loop. Instead of going through the vertical bar though you insert your hook under the horizontal bar, between the vertical bars. Make sure that you don't touch the vertical bars when doing this. Then you yarn over and pull up a loop as before.

Anyway, here are some basic patterns for you to try at home to make great gifts for your kids.

1. **Wrist Warmers**

We'll start with something every kid needs at some point; wrist warmers. These wrist warmers should end up being about six and a half inches long and two inches tall.

The materials you're going to need for this pattern are three different colors of medium weight yarn, a 5.5mm Tunisian crochet hook, a yarn needle, and a pair of scissors.

The gauge isn't very important with this pattern but to give you an idea 7 rows should be about 2 inches thick. The pattern makes two of the warmers, or enough for one kid, and is laid out below.

Row 1: Start by chaining ten with your first color. If you chain ten and it doesn't look tall enough you can chain a few more. Just remember to chain the same amount further down the line. Change to the second color in the last chain and simple stitch starting from the second chain from the hook, then in each chain across. Change to the third color at the beginning of the reverse pass, then change back to the first color in the last simple stitch of the reverse pass.

Row 2: Simple stitch in the second stitch from the hook and in each stitch across. Switch to your second color at the start of the reverse pass. Then switch to your third color at the last simple stitch of the reverse pass.

Row 3: Simple stitch in the second stitch from the hook and in each stitch across. Switch to your first color at the start of the reverse pass. Then switch to your second color at the last simple stitch of the reverse pass.

Row 4: Simple stitch in the second stitch from the hook and in each stitch across. Switch to your third color at the start of the reverse pass. Then switch to your first color at the last simple stitch of the reverse pass.

After that you need to repeat rows 2-4 seven more times at the least. Or just keep going until the wrist warmer is large enough for you. Then move on to row five.

Row 5: Slip stitch in the second stitch from the hook and in each stitch across. All you have to do after that is just finish off.

To make your button you need to use this pattern:

Round 1: Chain two then five sc in the second chain from the hook.

Round 2: Use 4 sc in the same chain, overlapping your previous round. Then finish off.

The strap is pretty easy. To do that you just have to chain six and then finish off.

To finish off the wrist warmers properly sew a button to one end of the wrist warmer and then sew the strap to the opposite end.

2. Miniature Hat Ornament

This great little hat is the ideal decoration for a Christmas tree, or just a wonderful little project for you to have a go at. The finished size of the hat is about 1 and three quarter inches across and high. You're going to need nine yards of worsted weight yarn, an I hook (that's 5.5mm) and a yarn needle. The gauge should be about four stitches for an inch but gauge isn't overly important here.

Here's the pattern:

Row 1: Chain sixteen and then skip the first chain. Pull up the loop through the back bump of each stitch so you have sixteen loops on your hook. Then yarn over and pull through one loop. Yarn over then pull through two loops and repeat that until only one loop is left.

Rows 2-8: Skip the first vertical bar. Insert the hook from the front to the back between strands of the next vertical bar. Yarn over and then pull up a loop. Repeat that across. To return you yarn over and pull through one loop. Then yarn over and pull through two loops until one loop is left.

Row 9: Skip the first vertical bar then insert the hook from the front to the back between strands of the next vertical bar. You yarn over, and pull up a loop, then repeat that across. To return just yarn over and pull the loop through all the other loops in the row, going one or two at a time. That's how you gather the crown of the hat. Finish off and then pull tight.

To finish you turn so the wrong side is facing and whipstitch the vertical edge closed. If you've done it right the bottom edge should flip up naturally. Secure the yarn to the inside of the crown and turn the right side out, and make a loop about three inches high. Knot the yarn near the crown, secure the yarn inside of the hat, and weave in all the ends. There you have it; one tiny little hat.

3. Tunisian Scarf

One common item that's made with crocheting is a scarf. Here's a look at just one of the many kinds of scarves you can make with Tunisian crocheting. Or, indeed, any kind of crocheting.

You're going to need 7 skeins of wool and a size J (6 mm) Afghan crochet hook. Remember Afghan crochet is just another way of saying Tunisian crochet. The gauge is that 14 stitches comes to about 4 inches.

To get started you need to work your foundation chain. For this pattern you need to chain 42 stitches. When you've made your foundation it's time to work with row 1.

Forward Row 1: Insert your hook through the space between the vertical strands, then yarn over and pull a loop through the hook. Insert the hook into the next space, yarn over, and pull the loop through onto the hook. Repeat that until you get to the last space, which needs to be skipped. Instead you insert your Afghan hook into the chain stitch at the edge. Pull the loop through onto the hook.

Return row 1: Chain one stitch, yarn over, and pull the loop through the next two stitches on the hook. Repeat until you get to the end, ending with one loop on the hook.

Forward row 2: Insert the hook into the second space, yarn over, and pull the loop through onto the hook. Insert the hook into the third space, yarn over, and pull the loop through onto the hook. Repeat that to the end of the row, including the last space. Insert your Afghan hook into the chain stitch at the edge, pull the loop through onto the hook.

Return row 2: Just do the same thing you did for the first return row. Then you just repeat these steps until the scarf is as long as you want it. The original pattern calls for 70 inches but that's way too long for a kid.

Now it's time for the finish.

This time when you do the first forward row insert the hook into the first space, yarn over, and pull through two loops on the hook. Repeat this until the end when you should have one loop left on the hook. Then you cut the yarn and pull through the remaining loop.

With the right side facing you, as you should for Tunisian crochet, join the yarn and make a single crochet into each stitch along the edge you're going to bind off.

Cut the yarn and pull through the remaining loop. Repeat that for the cast-on edge and then weave in all the ends and block how you want to finish completely.

4. Faux Knit Headband

This headband is great for keeping your kids heads warm and it's as soft as it looks.

You need two colorways of worsted weight yarn, a size J Tunisian crochet hook, and a yarn needle. Safety pins will help but aren't necessary. There isn't much of a gauge in this pattern either. Just keep going until it's the right size. You want to make one that's a few inches short because the yarn does stretch.

To begin with make a foundation chain nine stitches long using your first color.

Row 1: Work your forward pass in the first color. Drop the first color at the end and work your way back using the second color.

Row 2: Work the forward pass in the second color. Drop the second color at the end and work your way back using the first color.

Just repeat that until the headband is as long as you need it to be. When you finish the last row use a slip stitch in each stitch across.

When the headband is the right size it's time to finish it up. Cut the yarn, but leave a long trail of about ten inches long. Thread your yarn needle (you can also use a tapestry needle for this step) and stitch the two ends together. Weave in the ends and turn the headband right side out and you're good to go.

5. Crochet Beanie

Another common crocheted item is hats. This is one of the many kinds of hats you can make with Tunisian crochet.

You need one skein of soft wool, a size I Afghan hook, and a yarn needle. The gauge is that nineteen rows of nineteen stitches should give you a 5 inch square.

Row 1: Your foundation row needs to be a chain stitch of 36. Skip the first chain and pull up loops in the back bump of the other chains. Close by yarning over and pull through one loop on the hook. Yarn over and pull through two loops on the hook until you reach the end.

Row 2: Skip the first vertical bar. Working with a Tunisian full stitch insert your hook under the next 23 horizontal bars. Pull up a loop in each, giving you 24 loops on the hook. Close it by following the previous closing steps.

Row 3: Skip first vertical bar and first horizontal bar. Use a Tunisian full stitch and insert your hook under the next 23 horizontal bars, pulling up loops in each. Follow the same closing instructions.

Row 4: Skip first vertical bar. Working as for a Tunisian full stitch, insert the hook under the first horizontal bar and pull up a loop. Still working as for a Tunisian full stitch, insert hook under the next 16 horizontal bars, pulling up loops for each. Close the same as before.

Row 5: Skip first horizontal and vertical bars. Working as for Tunisian full stitch, insert hook under the remaining horizontal bars, even the ones from row 2-4. Pull up loops in each one too. Working as for Tunisian knot stitch, pull up a loop in the last vertical bar, giving you 38 loops on the hook. Close by yarning over and pull through one loop on the hook 7 times. Yarn over and pull through 3 loops on the hook 8 times. Yarn over and pull through 3 loops on hook. Yarn over and pull through two loops repeatedly until done.

Bind off by skipping the first vertical bar. Then, working for TFS, slip under each horizontal bar across. Then cut off the remaining yarn. With the yarn needle and about 18 inches of yarn seam the last row to the foundation row. Weave the yarn loosely along the edges of each row at the top of your hat using a different piece of yarn. Cinch gently to draw the hole together and sew it together to maintain the closure. Weave all the ends in securely and flip the hat "inside out" to finish.

6. Tunisian Crochet bookmark

This is a handy little bookmark for both kids and adults to enjoy their favorite books with.

You will only need a small amount of yarn. You'll also need a size G hook. You also don't need to worry about a gauge.

The foundation chain needs to be ten chain stitches long.

Row 1: Insert the hook into the second chain from the hook. Yarn over and draw up a loop. Insert the hook into the next chain, yarn over, and draw up a loop. Repeat until done.

Row 2: Insert hook under the second vertical bar of the previous row. Yarn over and draw up a loop. Insert the hook under the next vertical bar, yarn over, and draw up a loop. Repeat until done.

Row 3-38: Repeat row 2. At the end of row 38, with just one loop left, fasten off and sew in the end. You have a small little rectangle that makes an ideal bookmark.

7. Tunisian dishcloth

This is more one for kids to make than one made for kids, but here's a simple little pattern for a colorful dishcloth

You need 1 ball of white worsted weight cotton, 1 ball of pink worsted weight cotton, a size G Tunisian crochet hook, and a yarn needle.

Row 1: Use the white cotton to chain 25. Bring up a loop in each chain across. Yarn over and pull two loops up on the hook. Repeat that until back at the start.

Row 2: Insert the hook in the hump just above the next vertical bar. Bring up a loop. Insert the hook into the next vertical bar. Bring up a loop. Repeat that across and then finish as you did before.

Row 3-17: Repeat row 2. Then fasten off the white cotton.

Now to work on the perimeter.

Round 1: Join the pink cotton in the top right corner on row 17 sc. Chain 2 sc in that corner. Sc in each stitch going across, sc, chain 2, sc in the corner. Sc in each row down the left side. Sc, chain 2 in the next corner. Sc in each stitch across the bottom. Sc, chain 2, sc in the next corner. Sc in each row up the right side. Join it together using a slip stitch in the first sc you made.

Round 2: Slip stitch into the first chain 2 sc, chain three, dc, chain 2, 2dc in the same sp. Dc in each sc across. 2dc, chain 2, 2dc, in each chain 2 corner sp. Dc in each sc across. Repeat that around. Join with a slip stitch to the top of chain 3. Fasten off the pink cotton.

Round 3: Join the white in the same stitch as the slip stitch. Chain one. Sc in each next dc. 2sc, chain 1, 2sc in next chain 2 corner sp. Sc in each dc across. 2sc, chain 1, 2 sc in the next chain 2 corner sp. Sc in each dc across. Repeat that around. Join with a slip stitch into chain 1. Fasten off and then weave all the ends into the back of the work to finish.

Let's move on now to some more advanced patterns.

Chapter 5 – Advanced Patterns

In this chapter we'll be taking a look at some harder patterns. As long as you're familiar with the terminology and what you're doing you should be able to do these patterns.

8. Tunisian Crochet Cellphone Bag

Do your children have cell phones? If they do you can use this design to create a handy little bag for them to keep it in.

You need some size ten cotton thread in green and greensh grey. Or just two colors that fit well together. A 3.5 mm steel crochet hook. A sea shell bead, and some Velcro fastening finish the list.

To make the body use a double strand of green to chain 18 + 2. Use a basic Tunisian stitch on these 18 chains for 44 rows. Then fasten up.

The flap is a little more complicated. Join a double strand of greenish grey at the beginning of the last row and work on sc in each stitch across. Then turn.

Row 2: chain three, dec over next two sc, 1 sc in each sc across to the last sc. Then dec over the last two and turn.

Row 3: Chain 2, 1 sc in each sc across to the end. Turn.

Then you repeat row 2 and 3 until 2 sc remain. Pass the thread through both and fasten off.

For the strap you knit an I-cord using one strand of green and one strand of grey. You do this by using a pair of double pointed 3mm needles, cast on 3 stitches.

Knit across. Slide the stitches across the needle to the right edge and, bringing the thread to the right and behind the work, knit across again. Keep that up until the strap is as long as it needs to be and cast off the three stitches together to finish.

Finish the bag properly by sewing the sides together by using a weave stitch. Use the grey to crochet a row of sc along the margins of the flap. Attach the seashell bead to the top of the flap. Then sew the I-cord and Velcro fastening in place.

9. Tunisian Stitch Neck Warmer

This great little neck warmer is idea for keeping your loved ones necks warm in the cold weather.

You need two colors of medium weight yarn, a size I crochet hook, a yarn needle, and a pair of scissors. The gauge is that 7 rows should equal 2 inches.

Use the green yarn to chain 20, or as wide as you'd like the neck warmer to be.

Row 1: Work a simple stitch in the second chain from the hook, and in each chain across.

Row 2-53: Work the simple stitch in the second stitch and in each stitch across

Row 54: Work a simple stitch in the second stitch and in each stitch across. This time change to brown yarn in the last simple stitch.

Row 55-74: Work a simple stitch in the second stitch and then each stitch across.

Row 75: Work a slip stitch in the second stitch and then in each stitch across. Finish off.

To make the button (and you need to make two) just follow this pattern.

Row 1: Use the green yarn to chain 4, slip stitch in the forth chain from the hook to form a loop.

Row 2: Work ten sc in the loop.

Row 3: Work ten sc in the loop, overlapping the previous row.

Row 4: Work eight sc in the loop, overlapping the previous one again, and finish off.

To make the button strap, and again you need to make 2, use this pattern.

Row 1: Chain 15, then slip stitch in the first chain to form a loop, then finish off.

Use a yarn needle to sew the buttons onto the brown end of the neck warmer, and the button straps onto the green end.

10. Afghan Stitch Coaster

It's a small thing but a coaster can go a long way and makes for a fun small project and handmade gift. This pattern also features the long single crochet. To do this insert the hook into the stitch, yarn over, and draw a loop through to have two loops on the hook. Yarn over again, draw through both loops on the hook. These are really just regular single stitches but worked in a row that isn't the regular working row.

You need white and green worsted weight wool and a size G Tunisian crochet hook.

Row 1: Use the white wool to chain 14, draw up a loop in the second chain from the hook. Draw up a loop in each remaining chain. Yarn over and draw through the one loop.

Row 2-12: Draw up a loop in each vertical bar to get 14 loops on your hook. Yarn over, draw through one loop.

Don't fasten off right now.

Now to work the border.

Row 1: Use the soft white to chain 1, sc evenly around the entire coaster base (use the pattern sc, chain 1, sc) in each corner stitch. Now you fasten off.

Row 2: Join the green yarn in any stitch you want. Sc in some of the places you placed the single stitches in row one, working the singles as you go. Sc in each sc, with three sc in each corner.

Fasten off and you're done.

11. One Skein Scarf

Scarves are nice but they can use up a lot of wool. Here's a pattern that uses only one skein of wool. This pattern uses the Tunisian double crochet. Just yarn over, slide the hook from right to left under the post of the stitch, draw up a loop, yarn over, and pull through two.

You need one skein of homespun yarn and a 9mm Afghan hook.

Start by chaining 15.

Row 1: With one loop on the needle, use a simple stitch across the chain and do your return row.

Row 2: Chain two (this counts as your first double crochet), then double crochet across the row. Then return as before.

Row 3: Repeat row one and two until the scarf is as long as you want it to be. When you're done bind off using sc.

Yes it really is that simple.

12. Knit headband

This headband is great for keeping you warm in the cold weather. It's pretty simple to make too. This pattern uses the special instruction "Make 1". You do this by inserting the hook knitwise through the fabric in the space between the stitches. Pull up the loop after.

This pattern works with any yarn and needle combination so find one that fits for you.

Get started by chaining 5.

Row 1: Pick up each loop across

Row 2-5: Use a Tunisian knot stitch across the row

Row 6: find the centre stitch and knot stitch your way to it. Make 1, then knot stitch the centre stitch, make 1 again, then knot stitch your way across the rest of the row.

Rows 7-9: Knot stitch across the row.

Then just repeat row 6-9 until the scarf is 3.5 inches wide. Place a marker on the last increase row and measure the length from the beginning to that marker. Make a note of the measurement as "measurement A".

The total length of the headband should be about 18 inches. Remember that it's going to stretch when you put it on so it needs to be a few inches short. Double measurement A and subtract it from the size of the headband. This is measurement B and also needs to be noted. It'll be the main length of the headband. Continue in knot stitches across each row until you hit measurement B then it's time to start your decreases.

Row 1: find your centre stitch. Knot stitch across to one stitch before the center stitch. Skip that stitch and knot stitch the center stitch. Then skip the one after the center and knot stitch across the remaining stitches.

Row 2-4: Just knot stitch your way across the row

Repeat row 1-4 until only five stitches remain. Then complete one more row of knot stitches.

For the buttonhole row you need to find the center stitch again. Knot stitch across to the center stitch and skip it. Knot stitch from there to the end. On the return row you need to chain one for the skipped stitch.

Complete two more rows in knot stitches and bind off, and then fasten off to finish.

13. Ipod Hoodie

It's quite likely your kids have an iPod or iPhone. Because you use Tunisian stitches the hoodie is pretty thick and protective of whatever device they have.

You need sportweight cotton, and a size F needle.

To start with make a foundation of 14 chain stitches.

Row 1: Work your foundation row using simple stitch

Row 2: Work a row of knit stitches

Repeat row 2 until what you have is the size of your iPod and prepare to shape the collar.

The right side of the collar:

Row 1: Work a knot stitch in the first four stitches and finish as normal by leaving the rest of the row unworked. **Row 2** is an alternate to row 1 and what you do instead is work a knot stitch across while increasing between the last two stitches.

Row 3: Work a row of knot stitches

Row 4: Work knot stitches acrossing, increasing between the last two stitches

Row 5: Work a row of knot stitches

Repeat rows four and five until the number of loops is half of the number of chains you made in the first step.

Left side:

Join a separate piece of yarn into the unfinished row five stitches from the end. Work the same as you did on the right side but increase on the first two stitches, rather than the last two.

Then fasten off.

Pick up the stitch from the right side and work your way across the right side using knot stitches and across the left side.

Work in knot stitches until what you have fits up and over an iPod.

Hold the right sides together and then slip stitch the bottom, leaving an opening for the bottom port. Slip stitch up the sides.

Time to make the hood:

Chain an even number of stitches so that it fits around the opening. It should be around 18.

Work on even stitches using knot stitches for about eight rows and then decrease twice in the center of the next 2 or 3 rows.

Fold your work in half and whipstitch one side together for the top and then slip stitch the other end around the opening.

Lastly it's time to make the pocket:

Pick up a couple of stitches where you want your pocket to be and then work two rows of knot stitches. Then three rows decreasing at the beginning and end. Whipstitch the top down and you're done.

14. Kindle Cozy

Nothing like keeping a Kindle nice and warm between uses. Here's a handy little pattern to show you how.

You need two colors of worsted weight yarn and a MO-EZ hook. The gauge is that 6 rows should equal 2 inches.

You'll be using the Tunisian simple stitch for this. Start by chaining 18.

Row 1: Pick up a loop in every chain until the end (which is 18 loops) and do a basic return row on the way back.

Row 2-49: Pick up a loop in every vertical bar until the end (with 18 loops on the hook) and use a basic return row.

Row 50: Insert a hook through the next two vertical bars and pull up a loop. This is known as a decrease. Pull up a loop in each vertical bar until the last three stitches. Insert the hook into the next two bars and pull up a loop. Pull up a loop in the last stitch and use a basic return row.

Row 51: Repeat row 2.

Row 52: Repeat row 50

Row 53: Repeat row 2

Row 54: Repeat row 50.

Row 55 is the buttonhole row: Pull up a loop in each vertical bar for the first four stitches so you have five loops on the hook. Skip two bars and then pull up a loop in the remaining stitches, giving you ten loops on the hook. Return using a basic return except at the skipped stitches. With them you need to chain two and then complete the row.

Row 56: Pick up a loop in every vertical bar until the chain 2. Here you insert the hook into the space, making sure to go under the little bit of yarn made by skipping the stitch earlier. Pull up a loop and then keep pulling up a loop in the remaining bars. Use a basic return row.

Row 57: Repeat row 2

Row 58: This is the finish off row: Insert the hook into the vertical bar and pull up a loop. Pull the loop through the loop already on your hook, a slip stitch, and continue to the end of the row. If you're about to change color then finish off.

How to finish off: You need a kindle for this step. Or something the size of a kindle. Place the kindle on to the strip and then fold it over so you know where the sides meet. Hold the strip while removing the kindle to keep everything in place. Use a pin to help keep everything together. Take the second color and sc around the cozy, making sure you go through the thicknesses on both sides. It helps to start at the bottom of one side, go up and around the flap, and then down the other side. Now your kindle will always be nice and warm.

15. Knit stitch hat

We're finishing with another hat. This time it's a seamed hat that does wonders for keeping you warm.

You need two different colored sportsweight yarn, a J hook with the cable attached, and a tapestry needle.

Here's the pattern.

Chain 75 with your first color.

Row 1: With a loop on your hook, pick up each stitch across. Return your row like you normally would. Before you pull the hook through the last stitch you need to swap colors.

Row 2: Knit stitch across the row with a loop on your hook. Change the color on the last one of the return row again.

Row 3 onwards: Keep knitting across and repeating steps one and two, making sure to swap colors. Go until the piece is as long as you need it to be. Eight inches tall should give you a bit of a droop in your hat.

Decrease row 1: Knot stitch across each stitch. Yarn over on return row and pull through a loop. Yarn over and pull it through two more times. Yarn over and pull it through three. Yarn over and pull two three times, then yarn over and pull it through three. Repeat that step until you reach the end of the row.

Row 1A: Knot stitch across with your second color, sliding the hook through the decreased stitches in the last return row. That ensures that they stay decreased ones.

Decrease row 2: Knot stitch each stitch across. On the return row, yarn over and pull through a loop. Yarn over and pull through two, yarn over and pull through three. Then yarn over and pull through 2 three times, and yarn over and pull through three. Then repeat that step until the end of the row once more.

Row 2A: Knit stitch across with another color, making the hook through the decreased stitches in the last return row. This will make sure they stay decreased, as before.

Decrease row 3: Knit stitch across like with the other decrease steps. On the return row, yarn over and pull through one loop. Yarn over and pull through two, yarn over and pull through three. Then yarn over and pull through 2 three times, and yarn over and pull through three. Then repeat that step until the end of the row once more.

Row 3A: Knit stitch across with another color, making the hook through the decreased stitches in the last return row. This will make sure they stay decreased, as before.

Decrease row 4: Knit stitch each stitch across. On the return row yarn over and pull through three. Repeat the yarn over step until the end of the row.

Row 4a: Knit stitch across with another color, making the hook through the decreased stitches in the last return row. This will make sure they stay decreased, as before. There's no need to change color this time though. You should have fifteen stitches by this point. Cut the yarn, leaving a long tail of the last color used.

Time to finish up!

Thread the yarn through the tapestry needle and insert the needle on the left of the piece. It needs to go through the last row. Slide the needle through every stitch and pull the work snugly. The top of the hat must be gathered.

Turn the work over with the right sides and use the mattress stitch seaming it all together. After that you can get rid of the curling by blocking it or adding a brim. Or you can just accept it. Either way your hat is now complete.

Conclusion

So there you have it. You know the differences between crocheting and Tunisian crocheting, and you know how to make some great little gifts for your kids. We hope you've found all this educational and that your experiments with Tunisian crocheting succeed. Good luck!

Printed in Great Britain
by Amazon